STRUCTURAL TESTING USING CLOUD COMPUTING

DR.M.PARTHIBAN

Contents

I
INTRODUCTION TO STRUCTURAL TESTING

OVERVIEW OF STRUCTURAL TESTING

Structural testing is defined as the type of testing carried out to test the structure of Structural testing requires knowledge of the code and mostly done by the developers and concerned with how system tests rather than the functionality of the system and provides more coverage the testing. For example, to test the error message in an application, there is a necessity to test the trigger condition. Also, when testing the requirement which is drafted, sometimes the structural testing may miss out. However, structural testing aims to cover all the nodes and paths in the structure of There are three Structural testing techniques: i) Statement Coverage - This technique is aimed at exercising all programming statements with minimal tests. ii) Branch Coverage - This technique runs a series of tests to ensure that all branches are tested at least once. iii) Path Coverage - This technique corresponds to testing all possible paths, which means that each statement and branch is covered. Structural testing is complementary to Functional Testing and in this technique the test cases are drafted according to the system requirements which can be first , then more test cases are added to increase the test coverage. Structural testing can be used on different as unit testing, component testing, integration testing, functional testing etc. helps in performing a thorough testing software. The structural testing is mostly automated.

In structural testing the main problem is, the amount of defects in a software product can be very huge. The number of configurations of the product is greater, in testing bugs that occur infrequently and are difficult to find out. A rule of scan is that a system that is predictable to function without faults for a convinced length of time must have been previously tested for at least in that period which has simple significances for projects to write long survived reliable software. The practice of software testing is that a self-governing group of testers testing and conclude the software product by transporting it to the client. This practice frequently results in the testing phase, which is being used as a barrier to recompense for project postponements. Additional practice is to begin software testing at the same instant the project begins and it is a continuous procedure until the project completes.

The common practice of testing is for test suites to be established during technical support growth procedures in structural testing. Such testing is then continued in regression testing suites to safeguard that, upcoming updates to the software do not repeat any of the known faults, whereby testing defects found earlier can be overcome without much expense.

STRUCTURAL TESTING FOR CONVENTIONAL APPLICATIONS

Structural testing is about the quality of the system under test and it is necessary to focus on test case generated on code and finally produce the branch coverage. In addition, it is about the code and of the system to ensure project knowledge of the purposed system, such as its ability to perform and allow stakeholder to take decision about improvement, system quality and permit one to summit inside the box. In addition, it focuses particularly on using of the software to guide the selection of test data.

Different coverage methods used in white box testing are as follows: Code coverage implies each line of source code which has been executed. Function coverage means each function in has been executed. Debugging will always be white-box testing, where loops are of great problem. Integration testing is working modules and incorporating them. The modules should be tied together to form a particular system to understand how it works and know the information that is interfaced, as a result they are used to develop a system. In addition, it needs to make sure that the interface contains correct content and provides perfect testing.

In software testing automation, testing is the important key feature because testing is an extremely expensive mission in terms of instance and individual effort. In this automation, testing, structural testing plays a vital role in which an exact kind of program element is selected for branch coverage testing. In structural testing, the dynamic test data creation is the main functional approach for creating test cases because the creation is guided by the execution of the code under test. The total completion is achieved by any test case sets, which are usually known as coverage which reproduces the percentage of implementing structural elements like paths, branches, etc.

In earlier approach the information possible and impossible paths of the code in software testing. However, in structural testing, test coverage is designed as per the conditions of structural units that have been executed. These structural units can be branches, statements etc. Statement coverage is the division of the whole number of statements that have been implemented by the test data. In structural testing, branch coverage is the division of the whole amount of branches that have been implemented. In software program, the variable value is customized without the variable being modified along every path.

coverage, every time there are two or more feasible exits from the statement and it is known as . In software testing decision coverage testing is also known as branch coverage testing. There are two outcomes in statements either TRUE or FALSE along with the loop control statement like DO-WHILE or IF statement in a software program, the is either TRUE or FALSE. Each outcome of the branch coverage ensures at least performs TRUE and FALSE of control statement. Otherwise the research can say that control statement IF has been executed both to TRUE and FALSE.

The method to compute branch coverage is defined as follows: Branch Coverage = ((Number of branch outcomes executed / Total number of branch outcomes) *100%). In software testing, branch coverage processes the division of independent code segments which implements the measurement of decision outcomes. The independent code segments are segments of code that have no branches within or external of them. In addition, an independent code segment is a segment of code that is expected to execute in every instance when totally run. As per the recent surveys relating to software engineering, functional testing achieves only 60% to 90% branch coverage in software testing. Branch coverage testing is more successful than the statement coverage testing as well as it needs more test cases to reach 100% branch coverage. This research essentially focuses on branch coverage structural testing. The objective of this book is to advance existing structural testing methods that use evolutionary computing techniques like evolutionary algorithms, random testing, swarm intelligence, etc., to test case generation and constraint solving for calculating concrete test data. There are many methods used in the branch coverage testing of software, but they regularly require large computational cost and also complex algebraic manipulations which are overcome by proposed work C2IST.

Testing Methods for Conventional Applications

Adaptive searching techniques use genetic algorithms, which are illustrious from traditional methods, because they model the entire search space in addition to analyzing a fitness for each model, and then develop into a new set of models in an effort to produce a fitter test set. This procedure has been equated to the integration of genetic characteristics and therefore the name genetic algorithms emerged in addition to Darwin's theory of the survival of the fittest. Having generated a set of tests, the required test coverage of the software may be achieved by selecting a subset of the fittest tests using a model linear programming algorithm. A number of branches multifaceted program logics and produces tests to cover those needs with profound information the program structure and semantics. This research addresses this challenge with symbolic execution tools such as JPF, etc., discovers paths in the program under test symbolically and collects symbolic constraints at all branching points of an exposed path. The collected constraints are solved if feasible in addition to a key used to create a test that serves the execution of the program under test next to the path. This process is repetitive until all feasible paths are walked around or the amount of discovered feasible paths has reached the user-specified bound.

The function, which takes a explanation the problem as input and defines an output, is called fitness function. Control of fitness value is done frequently in a genetic algorithm and consequently it should be adequately fast. A slow computation of the fitness value can harmfully affect a genetic algorithm and make it extremely slow. In maximum cases, the fitness function and the separate function are the same as the objective is to either maximize or minimize the given isolated function. However, when the problem is more complicated with multiple constraints and objectives the designer different fitness function like symbolic execution. Symbolic execution is a structural testing technique where methodology explores feasible paths of the program under test by running the program with altered test inputs. This discovers a set of test inputs which is prime to the coverage of specific test targets.

Genetic algorithm

Genetic Algorithms (GA's) are of algorithm. Many potential solutions to the problems are created. Each solution is evaluated to see how it performs and these finest solutions are allowed to with each other. As Genetic Algorithm their genetic roots and the terms have accepted through into the computer equivalents. The initial population is created randomly with one hundred chromosomes and the individual populations are then evaluated. Every individual can collect a measure of its fitness in the environment which guides the reproduction. Recombination and mutation disturb those individuals, provided that general heuristics for searching. Recombination stage selected individuals are reproduced. To produce new individuals, the information's are exchanged in order. This information exchange is called crossover. Two selected individuals are combined to produce two new individuals at . the mutation stage, newly created individuals are changed lightly. Finally resulting individuals are then weighed through the fitness function. The fitness function estimates satisfies the test criterion.

Symbolic execution

Symbolic execution is a program analysis technique that executes programs with symbol rather than concrete inputs and maintains a path condition that is updated whenever a branch instruction is executed, to encode the constraints on the inputs that reach the program point. Using constraint solver, the test data generation is solved. For finding bugs the symbolic execution is also used to check run-time errors and it generates test inputs that trigger those errors.

In this research a new test data generation method is proposed in structural testing based on Genetic algorithm and Symbolic execution (GASE) which achieves high branch coverage. This book gives both theoretical and empirical analysis of structural testing to achieve high branch coverage. GASE proposes an uncomplicated technique that can obtain best results in time compared to other traditional techniques. The second investigation deals with GASE search based testing to improve efficiency and effectiveness in .

STRUCTURAL TESTING FOR WEB APPLICATIONS

Web applications have several user operations, which may produce many faults. These operations might be connected with one as a network. This network requires a collaborative technique for testing multiple tasks by detecting communicating operations.

is an essential task to make the web error free. Conventionally, testing team in an organization does manual inspections and uses defined rules for identifying faults in web applications. While, considering the dimension of increased users, the conventional method is very time consuming. Primarily, it is not possible to find all faults through manual inspection as the faults in web applications are in . The existing web application testing system simulates the multiple users, location etc. But it does not order the web applications efficiently based on their priority.

Testing Methods for Web Applications

Testing of web pages without ordering may result in of faults of critical applications in . For example, in a shopping website when payment page is not given first importance and home page a lot of importance in testing user interface and other tags, then the website will be a complete failure. This also leads to a question of what factors must be considered in prioritizing the applications and how to solve conflicts when multiple factors have . Not only ordering or prioritizing is also how fast ordering is carried is also an important factor, so of independent tasks must be implemented in order to execute prioritization in minimal time. All these issues must be sorted out in this web application testing framework. Testing web applications is an active area because of of end users, huge databases and many geographical locations are involved in it.

Web application testing over cloud uses cloud infrastructure. Testing organizations have many challenges such as more test cases, high payments per test, low test budget and no reuse of tests. To ensure high quality and to avoid outages, testing should be done within and outside the data . Unlike traditional on-premises testing environment, cloud testing provides users pay-per-use pricing, flexibility and reduced time. Manual web application testing is not time efficient, therefore testing environment should be automated in order to test the application efficiently. When this automated testing is carried out in , it adds an advantage, to minimize cost, time and resources. Hence the proposed system is used in the testing of web applications prior to its deployment by using cloud environment with prioritization, and Pareto-optimality ranking approach.

To develop an automated testing framework for web applications over cloud environment using Parallelization (simultaneous execution of multiple tasks), Pareto- of test execution to resolve conflict between multiple objectives (Based on Statement coverage, recent updating and execution cost) and Prioritization (detection of more faults in short duration) is required.

Web pages form the integral part of the web . The test cases written for web pages are taken as input for the testing framework. Web test cases consist of several operands that are used to form the basic functionality of each test case. Test cases are sorted and ordered based on the number of operands in each test case. The quantity of operands in each test case by utilizing the map reduce framework. The mapped class takes the operands in the test cases as the key and aggregated values are evaluated in the reduce class.

Prioritization

One of the major concerns in web testing is the distinguishing of the operands in the test cases, which are considered for test case prioritization and of the operands for calculating the execution time for each operand in each test case. The web testing framework involves of minimizing the execution time with utilizing map reduce framework. Dynamic method invocation in test cases may even pose a challenge to the web testing; it additionally faces issues in resolving conflicts between multiple objectives considered for Pareto optimality and having a balanced coverage between them.

Testing the web applications over the cloud environment also faces issues like modifying some of the test cases to suit the cloud environment, etc. The test outcomes would not be constantly reliable and precise due to the variations in network and internet services. Several cloud tools are designed for testing applications. They are to find a suitable cloud environment for testing web applications.

One of the major difficulties in testing over cloud is to detect each error in the web pages as the web pages take time to load with the poor bandwidth or slow speed. Thus, the testers experience frustration and can easily lose the interest in the web application. If the application contains any personal information of the user, then it does not provide enough freedom for the testing team to test the application.

When there are several limitations like time, , testing the quality of the website cannot be easily done and requires a lot of planning. Sometimes complexity increases with the limited time and cost for testing web-based applications. Another major problem is fetching the dynamic content of the web page as most of the contents of a web page come from different locations of the world, then there is a difficulty in reading the page source and detecting errors, since a page may have many pages as sources from where it fetched the data.

The testing process consists of more issues, but user faces an issue more than that the issues faced by the developer. In web development, the user must have the first interaction with the application to be as flawless as possible, allowing the user to adopt and use the application ease. Users can have experience testing web pages in all possible ways. The above mentioned issues are considered developing automated web application testing framework.

Cloud computing provides more ways of testing and it is beneficial to test an application in . The advantages of cloud testing are low costs, it involves only expenses and not capital expenses since the resources are provided by the cloud service provider. It also provides flexibility on demand like number of users, different platforms and browser versions and other factors can be simulated with minimum cost.

Cloud-based testing environments allow the testers to prevent when multiple users access at the same time. Test data can be generated during run time over cloud environment, which can be analyzed to detect faults. Runtime errors can be clearly visualized when they are tested in the development stage, as a result a lot of time and money can be saved before the application is deployed to the end user. Many websites fail to handle loads at peak time so when this case is handled properly, it reduces many problems and reduces negative feedback of the user. These factors are important to provide the developer and testing team freedom to carry out tests that are not limited by resources and capital.

Web applications are broadly classified into three main categories. (a) Browser based web applications (b) Client based web applications (c) Mobile based web applications. Browser based applications are the applications which contain JavaScript, jQuery, CSS and HTML tags. Client Based Web applications are mostly used in companies to transfer data between server and local systems. Mobile Web applications are used in cell phones, tablets, etc. They are specifically designed to overcome the limitations of small screen size, limited processing power and limited memory size of the mobile device.

Faults are major in browser based web applications since most of the requests require internet, whereas in client based web applications, only the basic queries of information retrieval are used between client and server. Mobile users spend most of the time in native and hybrid applications (combined features of both native and web applications) rather than the web applications. Even though most of the services provided by the website do not produce faults on a larger scale, minute faults may give rise to major problems. The end users might have a long lasting negative impact on the application if it is not properly tested.

STRUCTURAL TESTING FOR CLOUD APPLICATIONS

Recently, cloud computing and modifies an important realization in the way computation and services are provided to clients. Today's leading companies such as Amazon, IBM, etc., their cloud infrastructure for services. The cloud computing new business also grounds some major crashes on software testing and maintenance. The most important impact is known as testing as a service (TaaS). In cloud computing TaaS cloud infrastructures are measured as a new industry and service model. A provider assumes software testing of a given application system in a cloud infrastructure for clients as a service based on their demands. In cloud computing the TaaS is defined as a model of software testing used to test an application when a service is provided to clients crosswise the internet. allows daily operation, testing and maintenance support from side to side web-based browsers and servers.

Testing in the cloud or cloud testing can have the system under test which is available online and this strength may be called as SaaS software or non-SaaS software. In addition, this contains testing at unusual test levels like performance testing. Testing infrastructure and platforms are hosted transversely through different operation models of the cloud like public clouds, private clouds. Cloud environments should be tested and calculated for their availability, scalability, performance and security in order to support efficient delivery of services. A testing Cloud provides users with testing services such as auto generation of test cases based on different test criteria, test auto-execution, and test result evaluation. Test requests submitted by all the tenants are called as test tasks. Test tasks requested by different tenants have many worries, in the arriving time limit since the numbers of tasks are unidentified in advance.

Cloud Services Technology can be considered as the key technology for creation of Cloud Services. In modern years, cloud computing clients take advantage of lower expenses because of improved elasticity. provides services in a well-organized and scalable manner in addition to the cloud client's expense on a short-term pay per use basis. In Cloud Computing, Single Tenant Testing a single instance of the software and the complete supporting infrastructure works for a single customer. In the single tenancy each and every client has their own autonomous database and instance of the software and fundamentally there is no distribution process. Every person has their own and different instance from everybody. Single tenant gives improved security and each customer's data from any other customer. So there is limited possibility of one customer having rights to use another customer's data unintentionally.

can influence security built into databases to avoid and reduce hacking. Whereas multi-tenant systems require developing their own security systems to complete these similar benefits with the walls between data of dissimilar clients much thinner. It is a well-known fact that no system is 100% protected. A strong-minded hacker with significant instance and resources can crack through. The software task of the developer is to be confident enough to ensure, that the safety is strong or else it will not be significant for hacker's time. In multi-tenant applications reaching the threshold easier with low cost, since they are horizontal to security risks because each and every client's data exist within a single database.

Testing Methods for Cloud Applications

In early 1990's the public cloud services used an inheritance called a multi-tenant architecture. While structures and capabilities have changed, many , services are still grounded this 20th century architecture, which increases serious questions about how inheritance clouds prepare for disaster. While all architectures are vulnerable to hardware disappointments and other issues that source outages, the clouds that use multi-instance architecture can well minimize the influence of an outage.

Single tenant testing

Single tenant systems are regularly more consistent and the performance of one customer's system is not exaggerated by the events of other customers. If one customer's software behind while they are functioning on main complicated integration, e.g., if the software has bugs, to give up error and it does not involve in other customers' location, with the multi-tenant model when one customer event crashes all the other customers' event also crashes. Single tenant systems are easier to backup and restore customer databases, while each client database has its own separate backup. Multi-tenant can be frightening and do not offer this option. Multi-tenant systems often have boundary clients which are directly satisfied, has magnificent storage space and admittance boundaries. The Single tenant is easier to move around from SaaS to self-host. If a customer using a single tenant system wants to move from a SaaS environment into a self-hosted environment, the process is simple with little efforts. In case of the multi-tenant model it is difficult and is often unfeasible to move or enormously expensive to travel a self-hosted environment.

Single tenant systems are more elastic and allow customers to have an extensive range of customization choice by seeing database and software instances are single to each customer. In this research, with single tenant, they can be given contact the original code to modify and customize . In difference, the multi-tenant systems are frequently imperfect to the kinds of customizations and might be intelligent to modify the logo and colors in addition to setting up of some basic business rules or workflows. The multi-tenant system using a shared system and making changes to the platform is usually impossible. The single tenant provides control over upgrades. In a multi-tenant system, each and every client at one time a single push of new code. This is enormous for systems where all clients are doing the same thing; in addition, the users can provide accommodation and manage with some modification. In a single tenant system, each client has to upgrade independently and completely organize over when and how an upgrading takes place. They choose to delay or even skip development cycle when they approach in a busy time. over what time and how modernizing occurs is a good quality for nearly every one of our clients. The advantage of single tenant SaaS is solitude and there is only one instance a consumer. There are fewer threats of an additional trade either unintentionally or during company intelligence involved on data that does not feel right to them, since it is not possible to influence someone else's tasks. The single-tenant solutions are more accepted with venture businesses. Professions which involve exhaustive computing resources can make use of this system.

The drawbacks of Single Tenant SaaS are such that if a client makes a decision to run the cloud on premise mode, they must withstand the expenses of the whole system unaccompanied. A single-tenant system is normally costlier than a multi-tenant solution and normally does not have well-organized resources to use, because in a single-tenant system, each instance and the underlying software like operating system, run time libraries need to be restructured.

Multi- tenant testing

Multi-tenant SaaS applications are organized and implemented on multiple servers in a circulated technique. Multi-tenancy is defined as a single instance of the software take place the service provider's infrastructure; besides multiple tenants' accesses of the same hardware resources simultaneously. At the same time multi-tenancy is the organizational entity, which allows tenants to organize the SaaS application in the direction of fit to the needs as it runs on a complete location of all the tenants. In tenant groups have a number of users which are the stakeholders in the society. The bonus of the multi-tenant model is the deployment of , which fetches easily for the cloud service provider and also the multiple tenants, share the same hardware resources due to which the operation speed of the hardware is improved. Instead of installing hundreds of application instances only one be installed accordingly reducing the overall cost of the application.

Multi-tenant cloud computing platforms are constructed using an integrated database system for all customers. Multi-tenancy architecture was initially designed for customer service requests, running financial systems and mainly for airline reservations. As the number of customers in a multi-tenant cloud raised, a central database made it for cloud service providers to uphold the systems and to lodge the user development.

Multi-Tenant Testing is a web-based application testing in which it has a great quantity of open source tools that can be used. The tool of option depends on general solutions being developed. In multi-tenant testing the ideal approach would be an easy script that will implement the test and generate a report. The multi-tenancy is normal in design where a single instance of the software runs on a server, serving multiple tenants. A tenant is a collection of users sharing the same view the software they use. In the multitenant architecture, a software application is calculated to supply every tenant a passionate share of the instance together with its data and configuration in addition to the user management, tenant individual functionality where non-functional properties are involved.

In tenant collection for testing the clients, they utilize the foundation of characteristic or functionality. Generally, it is difficult to test every tenant it is required to model out tenants based on some boundaries. In testing tenant's exact data separation, the database, which classifies tenant data and authorizes data isolation, is preserved across various tenants. That is, one tenant data should not be observable to tenant. The characteristic separation is to legalize that any characteristic/functionality, which is controlled by one tenant, should not collide with the same characteristics on other tenants. In the API administration, all API'S inviting data from the system should be tenant conscious and a tenant modification at user level should be constrained. In multi-tenant testing all services should run for exact tenant and implementation of one batch task should only insert/adjust/remove data of that exact tenant. All integration services should be tenant conscious and should insert/modify/ remove data for their own tenant.

In data cleanse policy the elimination of one tenant from the system should not concern other tenant. Data should be inaccessible in such a way that cleaning does not generate trouble for other tenants. The cleaning should continue data isolation at various databases and browser level systems. Similarly, if a database from is performed from two different also the data isolation should be continued and the mechanism should run for multiple tenants in equivalent to each other tenants. This will imitate real time construction environment as much as they test tenant in equivalent for dissimilar functionality which are more protected towards practical breakdown. The corrupted data should not affect other tenant data and when there is an uncertainty running addition to it, this should not influence other tenant's performance. The individuality of the object is to authenticate for object exclusivity across the different tenants as no two objects, should get formed/customized/removed across tenants using parallel IDs. In tenants, file management is separated from database as there are some file system objects that need to be authenticated tenant exact view. Tenants should authenticate that; such file support resource should not be observable for the other tenant and intruders.

There are different SaaS development levels which are being introduced in Open Stack multi-tenancy cloud computing environment and relating to it is how the multi-tenancy cloud SaaS application is delivered to many tenants (customers). In the first stage of multi-tenancy, each customer has , which is customizable, and one host server, where every customer runs his or her own instance of the application. In the second level, each tenant has a separate instance of the application on the vendor host. In the third level, the vendor runs a single delivers each customer with configurable metadata and provides a single user experience and feature for each customer. In the fourth and final level of multi-tenancy, each tenant's separately among multiple customers on a load-balanced form having the same instance.

involved in structural testing

Structural Testing involves many challenges in manual testing as well as in automated testing. In software testing, it is complex to test complete application at once. There are millions of test combinations used in industries. When a project expands the regression testing work simply becomes uncontrolled by testers hence it is not possible to test each combination together in the manual as well as in automation testing. Whereby there exists pressure to handle the current functionality changes, previous working functionality checks, and bug tracking. Testing is always under time constraint, when tests software; they simply focus on task completion and not on the test coverage and quality of the work. The lists of tasks are high and testing cannot be done within specified time.

Conventional testing method with agile development is very familiar nowadays. Each day more teams are migrating to agile development, and it becomes important to understand how this approach changes effective testing teams. In software testing industry, due to continuous integration and changing is a possibility to miss critical tests for any requirement. This can be softened by linking tests to user stories for into test coverage and analyzing detailed metrics to detect and test coverage which are missed. Another cause of missing test coverage is due to change of code which was not projected. To moderate this, analyzing the source code is needed so as to identify segments that were changed to ensure all the segments of code are properly tested. Since code is transformed and composed for testing daily, the possibility of testing code may break in-between, which is much higher while manual testing. To handle this issue, of tests against each dimension is needed. Since most of the resources are constrained, it is impossible to test daily by testers, hence automated testing for testing code on is necessary. On the other hand, defects are significantly more expensive to fix later in the development cycle after manual testing. If is found at the time of requirements, it is cheaper to fix and has less effect on future coding than those found at the final stage in the testing cycle.

To resolve this issue, the testing team can do continuous code reviews to find the defects early, otherwise static analysis tools can be used to test the source code. This performs better in finding missing error routines, coding standard derivations, and data type mismatch errors. Nowadays all the software is designed with service oriented architecture that exposes APIs publicly, so that the other developers can extend the solution. For those who are developing APIs, it is difficult to overlook API testing because of the complexity involved. Normally testers who are having API's test skill are very less and they require strong coding skills. Hence, to avoid missing API tests, there are testing tools that allow testers to test the API without strong coding skills, from that testers will have to test whether these services are fully tested. As software becomes more mature, complexity normally increases. This difficulty adds more lines of code which introduces performance issues if the developer is not focused on how their changes have on end-user performance. To solve this issue, must know the program code issues that are affected and how performance can be improved over time. Load testing tools can help to detect slow areas and can check performance over time to document performance.

INTEGRATED STRUCTURAL TESTING APPROACHES FOR CONVENTIONAL AND CLOUD BASED APPLICATIONS - C2IST

The main objective of this research is to achieve performance testing. The performance testing is analyzed under three categories: initially for conventional then web and cloud based applications. In this book, a new conventional based structural testing method is proposed which integrates Genetic algorithm and Symbolic execution (GASE) which achieves high branch coverage also by providing both theoretical and empirical analysis of structural testing. GASE is a simple technique which can obtain best results in time compared to other traditional techniques and improves efficiency in .

Testing the web applications over the cloud environment also faces issues like modification of some of the existing test cases to suit the cloud environment. The test outcomes are not constantly reliable and precise due to variations in the network and internet services. Several cloud tools are designed at present for testing, which finds a suitable cloud environment for testing web applications.

Pareto optimality is a decision making technique used to satisfy conflicting objectives having equal importance. Web applications have several objectives of equal priority, which needs to be satisfied. Testing web the efficiency in optimizing these objectives. There is no single solution present at the same time that can optimize every objective for a non-trivial multi objective optimization issue. In those circumstances, there exists at least one Pareto optimal solutions fulfilling clashing objectives. A solution is called non dominated, Pareto optimal or non-inferior, if none of the objective function values are enhanced in a route without degrading some of the other objective values. All Pareto ideal solutions are considered equally best without the additional subjective preference data. Multi-objective optimization depends on Pareto optimality.

In the testing of the cloud based applications in , there are different SaaS development are introduced in Open Stack multi-tenancy cloud computing environment and measures to understand how the multi-tenancy cloud SaaS application is delivered to many tenants (customers). In the first stage of multi-tenancy, each customer has , which is customizable, and one host server. Every customer runs their own instance of the application. In the second level, each tenant has a separate instance of the application on the vendor host. In the third level, the vendor runs a single provides each customer with configurable metadata besides single user experience for each customer. In the fourth and final level of multi-tenancy, multiple customers run on a load-balanced form of the same instances through each tenant's which are maintained separately.

II

RELATED WORKS IN STRUCTURAL TESTING

SURVEY ON STRUCTURAL TESTING

In this book structural testing based on branch coverage testing is used. Branch coverage is a superset of statement coverage, which examines all parts of the program. Branches in the given program are the key elements in the branch coverage, thus, more importance is given to the branches. Branch coverage condition has a high potential value with respect to the software evaluation properties in the software.

Harman et al. (2011) analysed that "The most widely studied area of testing research that has been addressed using Search Based Software Engineering (SBSE) is structural testing. Harman proposed the program to measure coverage of some structural criterion. The most commonly considered criterion here is branch coverage, though other structural criteria have been confronted." Several papers have addressed the issue of test data generation with program-based structural criteria, referred to as program-based criteria.

In program based test data generation using meta-heuristic techniques, the basic approach is that of dynamic test data generation. The source code of the program under test is designed to collect information about the program as and when it executes. This is used to heuristically determine how close the test case is satisfying the specified test requirement as specified by the selected test criterion. This allows the test generator to modify the program's inputs gradually, moving them closer to the values that actually satisfy the requirement. In other words, the problem of generating test data enables us to understand the problem of function optimization. Further, such test generation methods handle arrays and pointer references because the values of array indices and pointers are known throughout the generation process. Wegener et al. (2010) specifies that because of the nonlinearity of software (conditional statements, loops, flags, switch-case, break), the conversion of test problems into optimization tasks usually results in complex, discontinuous and nonlinear search spaces for which search methods such as hill climbing are not suitable. To overcome such difficulty, meta-heuristic search methods can be deployed.

Korel et al.(1990), in his study on program-based test data generation describes a test data generation approach based on program execution, dynamic data flow analysis, and the function minimization methods. The test data generation problem is reduced to a sequence of sub-goals. Function minimization methods are also used to solve the sub-goals. Moreover, dynamic data flow analysis is applied to speed up the search process by identifying the input variables that influence undesirable program behaviour. Korel et al.(1990) describes two approaches for test data generation: random and path-wise. They also introduce the concept of dynamic test data generation for node coverage criterion, critical branch and sub-goals. Whereby the program behaviour is analysed from their study and a dynamic model for testing any type of program is proposed in this book.

RELATED WORKS ON STRUCTURAL TESTING FOR CONVENTIONAL APPLICATIONS

Arcuri et al.(2012) analysed that the length of test sequences plays an important role in testing software with internal state. In particular, they concentrate on the branch coverage criterion because it is one of the most important common criteria in the literature. This approach has two main issues; first it has to decide how long to apply random testing. Next, when the target specific branches have to decide on how much effort it takes to cover them. There are cases where a single test sequence will cover all the feasible branches which do not exist. The proposed GASE provides solution for overcoming such issues and branch coverage is improved providing high coverage percentage of branches.

Baars et al. (2011) presents an algorithm that combines symbolic execution with dynamic analysis to improve search based testing efficiency. The statistical analysis is not more efficient when reusing symbolic information for nested branches. Hence, enhanced fitness function GASE is used in the proposed work, to achieve high branch coverage and to make search based testing more efficient.

Bertolino et al. (1994) discussed a general algorithm that covers path for a given program flow graph. They showed a reduced flow graph called DD graph and practiced graph theoretic principles. Also, they have done experimentation on path finding using prototype tool in laboratory. Experiments were not carried out for real-world programs and for evaluating the performance of branch coverage testing. In this book GASE testing is proposed for achieving high branch coverage with different branches of programs and compared with existing branch coverage tools.

Chusho.T (1987) proposed a new coverage testing tool, created on the number of essential branches performed at least once by test runs of a program. The main drawback in this work is that only essential branches are covered while testing and the results show only 60% branch coverage. Whereas the proposed branch coverage GASE covers all branches and achieves higher branch coverage compared with the testing tool proposed by Chusho.

Baddeti et al. (2013) proposed an efficient CBIR system based on Genetic Algorithm for retrieving relevant images from image database, when a query image is provided. McMinn et al. (2004) investigated the relationship between search space size and search performance and the ability of a search technique to find the test data and its evaluation. Their research used the irrelevant input variable removal strategy as a means of reducing input domain dimensionality for search-based structural test data generation techniques which has been overcome in the proposed work.

Chen et al. (2013) evaluated and compared the performance of adaptive random testing and random testing with perspective of code coverage. At the same time Chen et al. exposed wide range of investigations, in terms of higher code coverage which brings higher breakdown recognition potential, to get better effectiveness of software dependability evaluation. GASE, when compared with 13 classes of program which contains low to higher code coverage, proved to have higher branch coverage.

Chen et al. (2004) proposed an Adaptive random testing that improves the fault-detection capability. This work increased the adaptability of random testing when compared to other existing branch coverage testing algorithms. GASE algorithm is adaptable for larger programs and improved branch coverage than existing branch coverage algorithms.

Jones et al. (1998) applied GA (Genetic Algorithm) successfully to several problems, varying in complexity from a quadratic equation solver to a generic sort module that comprised several procedures. In these cases, full branch coverage was not obtained due to constraints. The quality of the test data was enhanced by designing the fitness function to generate data close to a sub domain boundary where the likelihood of revealing an error was higher. The proposed GASE integrates GA (Genetic Algorithm) and SE (Symbolic Execution), here SE is mainly for analyzing the program to execute, assign symbolic values rather than actual values and solve constraints for the possible outcomes of each conditional branch.

Ntafos et al. (1988) compared a number of structural testing strategies in terms of their relative coverage of the program's structure and also in terms of the number of test cases needed to satisfy each strategy. They also discussed some of the deficiencies of such comparisons. The common test case written in GASE is that the feasible paths are fully covered and infeasible paths are not covered, whereby producing higher branch coverage.

Taylor et al. (1992) extended the notion of structural testing criteria to concurrent programs and proposed a hierarchy of supporting structural testing techniques. Coverage criteria description included concurrency state coverage, state transition coverage, and synchronization coverage. Requisite support tools included a static concurrency analyser having either a program transformation system or a powerful run-time monitor with the help of controllable run-time scheduler. The techniques proposed were only suitable for Ada or CSP languages and results were obtained for programs having only static naming of tasking objects. The proposed GASE is suitable for all languages having main class programs and can be used dynamically.

RELATED WORKS ON STRUCTURAL TESTING FOR WEB APPLICATIONS

The main objective of testing the web applications is to overcome the occurrence of the faults. Finding more faults in minimum time is achieved through test case prioritization process. Nayak et al. (2016) found that in most situations, test case prioritization process was carried out based on faults. There are also several techniques for prioritizing the test cases. In the survey on web applications in testing, researchers have analyzed the difficulties in the existing approaches.

Srikanth et al. (2016) used BAT (Build Acceptance Test) technique to validate the quality of a software system every time a build was generated. Three important techniques of test case prioritization were proposed in this work. The first technique considers the number of tasks involved in web applications and the web pages with the maximum number of tasks dominating the one with the lower number of tasks gaining highest priority. The second technique concentrated on historically failing tasks. That is accounting, when a particular task has failed for large number of times. The third technique was based on greedy approach which tested new tasks each time it encountered it; instead of testing previously tested tasks assuming that the tasks which were not tested earlier were likely to produce more faults than the tasks which had been tested previously. When the number of tasks is considered, if there is a tie between the test cases which have same number of tasks, then there will be confusion as to which test case gains more importance. For newly designed software history of failures cannot be collected.

Chawla et al. (2016) proposed Genetic Algorithm (GA) and Particle Swarm Optimization (PSO) algorithm which are similar to natural selection process. This technique is based on biological evolution where the test cases are selected and by mutation and crossover different combinations are made and fitness function is calculated. This algorithm encodes the test cases into some data structures called Chromosomes. A selection operator is used to select two best combinations from the set of test cases and combines these two to form a new test case. Then mutation is performed in the new test case by interchanging the order of operations within the test case. Particle Swarm Optimization (PSO) is a test case generation and reduction technique that optimizes a problem by optimizing candidate solution in a step by step manner by considering quality of the test case. Even though test cases are generated by selection and mutation vital factors like execution cost, execution time etc., they are not considered.

The particle representation contains not only parameter values but also the constructor and method invocations. The Gbest molecule set is shaped from the Pareto fronts and PBest are the particles that have better Pareto positions. Pareto ideal test suite acquired in this way is additionally limited and organized by the mapper; lastly JUnit record is produced. Similarly, in the proposed framework is the efficient test case generation for more than one object. Pareto optimality is one which satisfies multi-objective functions and parallelization through the design of map reduce framework. In this work statement coverage, execution cost can also be considered while generating test case, also test case prioritization can be performed on the generated test cases so that vital test case which is likely to produce more faults are executed first.

El Youmi et al. (2014) consolidated an approach using Fuzzy testing and all-pairs testing methods to boost the viability of testing web applications. The hybrid approach called Fuzzy All-pairs testing is empowered to distinguish mistakes and bugs coming, because of blends of classes of sources of information. To assess this approach, Equivalence Partitioning and Boundary Value Analysis were compared utilizing three distinct sites. This exact review demonstrated that this approach recognized a larger number of defects than Equivalence Partitioning and Boundary Value Analysis. The basic idea behind test case reduction is extracted from their research. The testing is to take a page that demonstrated a problem and reduce as much as test cases as possible while still reproducing the original problem for testing. Fuzzy technique used random generations of test cases and identified only simple faults. All pair's technique involved testing all the possible combinations, which requires more storage space and time.

The hybrid approach called Fuzzy All-Pairs Testing is a test case detection technique that enables us to detect errors and bugs based on pair wise identification by partitioning. This technique was demonstrated by testing a telephone number whether a given telephone number is valid or not. Here, instead of testing for all possible combinations of telephone number, the number was split into pairs and only valid combinations of a particular pair was tested minimizing the number of test cases. Fuzzy All-Pairs technique detected more errors than Equivalence Partitioning and Boundary Value Analysis and it also reduced the number of test cases. In this book test case reduction technique, prioritization is on the reduced test cases.

Martino et al. (2013) implemented a decent testing structure, which could diminish the coupling among the test modules, enhance the test effectiveness and scope rate, which decreased the cost and guaranteed the software quality. In this book the structure of the web application automatic testing framework was based on selenium. Initially, testers could create test cases by filling template. These test cases could create the unit testing code through the Administrative Terminal System (ATS) working stage. ATS operating platform was divided into four basic areas. They include case selection area, command detail area, command edit area, and command description area. This framework required the generation of fully tested code according to the test case. The specific requirements include simple interface, comprehensive function and stable code. The function modules in automated testing process were data input module, template module, command class module, code generation and automatic compilation module. The testing process was automated using selenium by generating a testing environment.

The proposed book has the advantage of not only determining the testing language, but also it determines the kind of browser utilized for testing. If browsers are not specified, each test document would be created in the program as a unit. Thereafter, automated saving, compilation, and operation were implemented through the version control and continuous integration server. Finally, the results were reported to the testers using XML or Excel. Even though automatic code generation was effective, execution cost and number of tasks involved in test cases had to be considered. The test cases were also ordered in order to identify maximum faults in minimum time duration.

Justus et al. (2015) presented an automated method for testing web applications that required content contribution from clients. The proposed procedure investigates the pages of a web system. When a page that required content information was experienced, this testing technique checked the test information bank for suitable case individual profile information to encourage it into the content information fields of the page. Exploratory outcomes demonstrated that this system could consequently go through Site pages that questioned information and client account recognizable proof. The testing procedure would automatically scan the information in the web pages and deduce input test data to either test the syntax of those input fields or send the web pages which need complicated user data. This procedure first scanned the pages of a web program that built a state-transition diagram of the web application. In the diagram, the states were the pages while the edges were transition between pages. After this, the clients might check the state transition diagram and spot activities that were deflected due to inappropriate input data. This testing system then found appropriate test input from the test data bank for this activity. The system would rescan the pages after the input test data were generated for appropriate actions.

The testing system may repeat these two steps until either the budget of testing runs out or the required test results are obtained. Test case regeneration is used to increase the diversity of workload to the web program. Here, the user information is used in the testing framework for processing. As a result, privacy of the user information must be considered. Only invalid input is considered but the webpage response in different browsers and platforms, broken links etc. are not considered. Test case is generated but not prioritized.

Kuk et al. (2008) proposed the Cluster application as a productive way to deal prioritization. Test case in the same group was considered to have comparative practices. This paper proposed assemble clustering algorithm because the Agglomerative Hierarchical Clustering (AHC) could adequately manage the unpredictable informational collections that was not regular. Prior to the clustering, they first made the faults and then the code that was involved in the process is predicted and the corresponding outcome of the process was also predicted. They performed intra cluster prioritization wherein the test cases within the same cluster were prioritized and also inter cluster prioritization wherein test cases in different clusters were prioritized.

This approach was not used for test cases, which involved sequential operations as in many situations where one data was dependent on other data as this approach divided tasks in test cases and also vital factor like time taken for execution of test cases. Even though they considered KLOC (line of codes) and number of class files, they had not provided an approach to resolve between conflicts in multiple factors as both the factors KLOC and number of class files had equal importance. The author had compared with K means algorithm and proved that there was a significant increase in average percentage of faults detected but this algorithm had not been compared with the existent clustering algorithms like K means and also not compared with non-clustering algorithms.

A two-stage approach was proposed by Dawei et al., (2016) to produce test cases naturally by breaking down the structure of the Internet application. The reliance connections, information reliance and control reliance, in the Internet application were characterized and the connections were distinguished from source code, the experimental method was enhanced with the investigation result. A novel approach for automatic test case generation for web applications was implemented in a prototype tool. This process included generation of test cases, extraction of dependencies and maintaining data dependency and control dependency for test case reduction when there were large numbers of test cases under the situation of state explosions. Finally, the test case reduction approach was experimentally evaluated for better efficiency and effectiveness for web applications.

Web applications test cases were designed using Ajax environment with java script and dynamic DOM structure. The test cases were executed automatically in selenium environment. A novel approach was introduced for the automatic test case generation in web application. Then, the data and control dependencies existing in web applications were observed and the characteristics of the dependencies were applied to the web applications. The data and control dependencies were extracted from the source code and analyzed for test case generation. Data dependency was defined when there was a transfer of data from source page to destination page in web application. Control dependency was defined by the links in conditional or loop statements in a web page. Total execution cost and the number of tasks should also be considered in test case reduction in addition to data dependency and control dependency.

The test case prioritization is essential in minimizing the time required for testing web applications. Several techniques for test case prioritization have been discussed in this chapter. The test cases have also been prioritized based on fault severity. The fault severity plays a major role in ordering the test cases. Multiple criteria have been analyzed in prioritizing the test cases. Coverage of those criteria has been taken into account for improving the efficiency of the test performance.

Random algorithms have also been used for prioritizing the test cases for web applications. Proportion oriented randomized algorithm (PORA) has been used for prioritizing the test cases by grouping the similar test cases. But PORA finds it difficult to generate scenarios on real time basis without manual intervention. Test cases can also be prioritized using regression testing through optimization algorithm, Cuckoos Search (CS) algorithm. It selects and prioritizes number of faults covered in minimum time though it is not always efficient due to random grouping of test cases.

RELATED WORKS ON STRUCTURAL TESTING FOR CLOUD APPLICATIONS

Cloud computing researchers began to pay attention to testing as a service in a cloud environment from the year 2010 onwards. A number of research papers have addressed this Testing as a Service (TaaS) subject in different outlooks. Several papers have discussed about SaaS Testing or Multi-Tenant Testing.

Abbadi et al. (2013) proposed a novel cloud scheduler which analyses both infrastructure properties and user requirements. Also they present their prototype built on Open Stack and proves the scheduler by trustworthy input in relation to the trust status of the cloud infrastructure.

Chaisiri et al. (2012) proposed an optimal cloud resource provisioning algorithm to stipulate resources accessible by several cloud providers. In addition, they formulate and determine integer programming with multistage remedies to get optimal solution. In the proposed Multi-inhabitant testing, every single occupant execution are broke down to accomplish ideal arrangement.

According to Corradi et al. (2014) Virtual Machine (VM) consolidation has to be carefully regarded as the combined resource utilization of additional VMs to prevent performance reductions and service level agreement violations. Corradi et al. (2014) focused from a more practical viewpoint regarding the exact attention on the consolidation portions associated to power, CPU, and networking resource sharing. In addition, the work suggests a Cloud management platform to optimize VM consolidation in three main dimensions: power consumption, host resources, and networking.

Du et al. (2014) proposed Int-Test that was an efficient service and scalable integrity attestation framework for SaaS clouds. They provided a novel integrated attestation graph analysis scheme. This graph analysis provides a strong attacker systematic power than earlier methods. In addition, it automatically improves result quality by replacing bad results formed by malicious attackers with high-quality results created by gentle service providers in cloud environment. In this book the proposed Multi-tenant performance testing using GASE algorithm achieves the tenant's fitness function to achieve performance for producing high quality results.

In the recent past, Salesforce.com has built-up software services over the cloud that is affordable. This company provides policy for customer relationship managements and contains Service Cloud that plan to support creation, tracking and routing of customer cases. In addition, it provides App Exchange which is based on marketplace concept to provide web application for clients and Collaboration Cloud to connect among employees within organizations. Krebs et al. (2013) performed the evaluation in a realistic environment, which widely exists and accepted. Transaction Processing Performance Council Web e-commerce (TPCW) benchmark was enhanced with Multi-tenancy support Transaction Processing Performance Council Web e-commerce (MT-TPC-W).TPC-W was previously used before in multi-tenant performance isolation situations. MTTPC-W is an online bookstore which follows numerous online browsers in which the workload is dynamically generated by accessing web pages.

Multi-tenancy differentiates between requests originating from different tenants by isolating their information, producing a closed round workload whereby one online browser performs like a user which is characterized by a think time and a Markov Chain describing the request flow. Samba (2012), who has defined a hybrid model, manages to bridge both Distributed Management Task Force (DMTF) and National Institute of Standard Technology (NIST). These standards offer high-level reference architecture for the management of clouds and are not selective sufficient to be executed as such with gaps in the lower levels that need to be filled with other specifications.

Calero et al. (2014) described an authorization model which facilitated the organization with features for instance role-based access control, hierarchical, conditional and hierarchical objects. This access control model took benefits in logic formalism suggested by the Semantic Web technologies to illustrate the underlying infrastructure and the authorization model. In addition, these rules are employed to protect the access rights from the resources in the cloud. This model is particularly planned by taking into consolidation of the multi-tenancy nature environment. In addition, a trust model that accepts fine-grained information, which is accessible by individual tenant, is formulated. Their study is utilized in this proposed work for defining the behaviour of tenants.

Vashistha et al. (2012) analyzed two major approaches to improve the data isolation between the tenants. First approach is process isolation, where data in a multitenant organization is suspiciously treated so that it could be mixed with another user. The second approach is the effective decryption technique which deals with user data which is needed to be read by the intended users, but should not be converted by the others. The above research has been done with cryptographic techniques enabling selective decryption. In the proposed book, the challenges of performance testing are addressed in the multi-tenant SaaS applications using Open stack Ubuntu 15.04.

Solis et al. (2014) showed that the performance of public and private clouds themselves varies for different resources, across the data centre, and over time. Such variability affects for the low latency streaming applications, and forced to use adaptation algorithms. Hence dynamic structured testing is proposed for testing cloud applications.

The main objective of testing the web applications is to overcome the occurrence of the faults. Finding more faults in minimum time is achieved through test case prioritization process. Nayak et al., (2016) found that in most situations, test case prioritization process was carried out based on faults. There are also several techniques for prioritizing the test cases. In the survey on web applications in testing, researchers have analysed the difficulties in the existing approaches.

Srikanth et al. (2016) used BAT (Build Acceptance Test) technique to validate the quality of a software system every time a build was generated. Three important techniques of test case prioritization were proposed in this work. The first technique considers the number of tasks involved in web applications and the web pages with the maximum number of tasks dominating the one with the lower number of tasks gaining highest priority. The second technique concentrated on historically failing tasks. That is accounted, when a particular task has failed for large number of times. The third technique was based on greedy approach which tested new tasks each time it encountered it instead of testing previously tested tasks assuming that the tasks which were not tested earlier were likely to produce more faults than the tasks which had been tested previously. When the number of tasks is considered, if there is a tie between the test cases which have same number of tasks, then there will be confusion as to which test case gains more importance. For newly designed software, history of failures cannot be collected.

Chawla et al. (2016) proposed Genetic Algorithm (GA) and particle swarm optimization (PSO) algorithm which are similar to natural selection process. This technique is based on biological evolution where the test cases are selected and by mutation and crossover different combinations are made and fitness function is calculated. This algorithm encodes the test cases into some data structures called Chromosomes. A selection operator is used to select two best combinations from the set of test cases and combines these two to form a new test case. Then mutation is performed in the new test case by interchanging the order of operations within the test case. Particle Swarm Optimization (PSO) is a test case generation and reduction technique that optimizes a problem by optimizing candidate solution in a step by step manner by considering quality of the test case. Even though test cases are generated by selection and mutation vital factors like execution cost, execution time etc., they are not considered.

The particle representation contains not only parameter values but also the constructor and method invocations. The Gbest molecule set is shaped from the Pareto fronts and PBest are the particles that have better Pareto positions. Pareto ideal test suite acquired in this way is additionally limited and organized by the mapper; lastly JUnit record is produced. Similarly, in the proposed framework are efficient test case generation for more than one object, Pareto optimality that satisfies multi-objective functions and parallelization through map reduce framework is designed. In this work statement coverage, execution cost can also be considered while generating test case, also test case prioritization can be performed on the generated test cases so that vital test case which is likely to produce more faults are executed first.

El Youmi et al. (2014) consolidated an approach using Fuzzy testing and all-pairs testing methods to boost the viability of testing web applications. The hybrid approach called Fuzzy All-pairs testing empowered to distinguish mistakes and bugs coming, because of blends of classes of sources of information. To assess this approach, Equivalence Partitioning and Boundary Value Analysis were compared utilizing three distinct sites. This exact review demonstrated that this approach recognized a larger number of defects than Equivalence Partitioning and Boundary Value Analysis. The basic idea behind test case reduction is extracted from their research. The testing is to take a page that demonstrated a problem and reduce as much as test cases as possible while still reproducing the original problem for testing. Fuzzy technique used random generations of test cases and identified only simple faults. All pair's technique involved testing all the possible combinations which requires more storage space and time.

The hybrid approach called Fuzzy All-Pairs Testing is a test case detection technique that enables us to detect errors and bugs based on pair wise identification by partitioning. This technique was demonstrated by testing a telephone number whether a given telephone number is valid or not. Here, instead of testing for all possible combinations of telephone number, the number was split into pairs and only valid combinations of a particular pair was tested by minimizing the number of test cases. Fuzzy All-Pairs technique detected more errors than Equivalence Partitioning and Boundary Value Analysis and it also reduced the number of test cases. In this book test case reduction technique, prioritization is on the reduced test cases.

Martino et al. (2013) implemented a decent testing structure, which could diminish the coupling among the test modules, enhance the test effectiveness and scope rate, which decreased the cost and guaranteed the software quality. In this book the structure of the web application automatic testing framework was based on selenium. Initially, testers could create test cases by filling template. These test cases could create the unit testing code through the Administrative Terminal System (ATS) working stage. ATS operating platform was divided into four basic areas. They included case selection area, command detail area, command edit area, and command description area. This framework required the generation of fully tested code according to the test case. The specific requirements included simple interface, comprehensive function and stable code. The function modules in automated testing process were data input module, template module, command class module, code generation and automatic compilation module. The testing process was automated using selenium by generating a testing environment.

The proposed book has the advantage of not only determining the testing language, but also it determines the kind of browser utilized for testing. If browsers are not specified, each test document would be created in the program as a unit. Thereafter, automated saving, compilation, and operation were implemented through the version control and continuous integration server. Finally, the results were reported to the testers using XML or Excel. Even though automatic code generation was effective, execution cost and number of tasks involved in test cases had to be considered. The test cases were also ordered in order to identify maximum faults in minimum time duration.

Justus et al. (2015) presented an automated method for testing web applications that required content contribution from clients. The proposed procedure investigates the pages of a web system. When a page that required content information was experienced, this testing technique checked the test information bank for suitable case individual profile information to encourage into the content information fields of the page. Exploratory outcomes demonstrated that this system could consequently go through Site pages that questioned information and client account recognizable proof. And, to ensure privacy of the user information only invalid inputs are considered but the limitation is webpage response in different browsers and platforms, broken links etc. are not considered, also test case is generated but not prioritized. In the proposed work this limitation is overcome by prioritization.

Kuk et al. (2008) proposed the Cluster application as a productive way to deal prioritization. Test case in the same group was considered to have comparative practices. This paper proposed assemble clustering algorithm because the agglomerative hierarchical clustering (AHC) could adequately manage the unpredictable informational collections that was not regular. Prior to clustering, they first made the faults and then the code that was involved in the process is predicted and the corresponding outcome of the process was also predicted. They performed intra cluster prioritization wherein the test cases within the same cluster were prioritized and also inter cluster prioritization wherein test cases in different clusters were prioritized. This approach was not used for test cases, which involved sequential operations as in many situations one data was dependent on other data as this approach divided tasks in test cases and also vital factor like time taken for execution of test cases. Even though they considered KLOC (line of codes) and number of class files, they had not provided an approach to resolve between conflicts in multiple factors as both the factors KLOC and number of class files had equal importance. In their work there was a significant increase in the average percentage of faults detected but this algorithm was not compared with the existent clustering and non-clustering algorithms.

A two-stage approach was proposed by Dawei et al., (2016) to produce test cases naturally by breaking down the structure of the Internet application. The reliance connections, information reliance and control reliance, in the Internet application were characterized and the connections were distinguished from source code, the experimental method was enhanced with the investigation result. Based on their study in this work, a novel approach for automatic test case generation for web applications was implemented in a prototype tool. This process included generation of test cases, extraction of dependencies and maintaining data dependency and control dependency for test case reduction when there were large numbers of test cases under the situation of state explosions. Finally, the test case reduction approach was experimentally evaluated for better efficiency and effectiveness for web applications.

NEED FOR INTEGRATED STRUCTURAL TESTING APPROACH

Testing includes software components, hardware components, or together are combined and tested. Testing evaluates an interaction between these two components. Integration testing usually goes through several real world business scenarios to see whether the system can successfully complete workflow tasks. The order of combining the modules into partial systems is called an Integration plan. In structural testing, testing all decision outcomes within a module independently, at the integration level focuses on the decision outcomes that are involved with module calls. The design reduction technique helps to identify those decision outcomes, so that it is possible to exercise them independently during integration testing.

Works Related to Integrated Structural Testing

In software testing the critical task is the creation of test data to satisfy a given test - coverage criterion. This process is called as Test Data Generation. Automated testing requires automatic test data generation. Developments in the field of 'automated test data generation' was initiated in early70's when papers on "Testing large software with automated software evaluation systems" by Rama moorthy, in 976 and Holland, in 1975 and "Automatic Generation of Floating-Point Test Data" by Miller and Spooner, in 1976 were published. Clarke, in 1976 was the first person to produce a solid algorithm for Automatic Test Data Generation (ATDG).

Bryce (2006) explained about various existing mechanisms to deal with complex testing problems. The main problem is classifying an important prerequisite to the selection of a suitable solution strategy. Information regarding problem complexity and existing algorithms provide useful points for new algorithm development. Automatically test data generation for software testing with minimum time and cost is known to be NP-hard and only exhaustive search guarantees the optimal solutions, but these can become too much expensive to compute even for small problems. Several methods have been used to solve combinatorial optimization problem but each of them has its own limitation and advantages. Some of the surveys specify useful optimization techniques to solve the software testing problems and software test case generation for software testing. Survey ranges from traditional exact methods to modern meta-heuristic methods.

Wegener (2001) proposed a number of test-data generation techniques which have been developed for coverage of software under test. Test adequacy criterion usually involves coverage analysis, which can be measured based on different aspects of software like statements, branches, paths and all-uses. In statement testing, each and every statement of the software/ program under test has to be executed at least once during testing. The main drawback of statement testing is that even if one achieves a very high level of statement coverage, it does not reflect that program is error free.

Chilenski (1994) explained that branch coverage is stronger testing criteria than statement coverage testing criteria. The novelty is each and every branch has to be executed at least once during branch coverage testing. In this testing all control transfer are executed. Only few errors can be detected if the statements and branches are executed in a certain order.

Frankl (1998) have generalized & extended the comparison studies on random testing vs. partition testing to that of operational testing vs. debug testing. The statistical measure they have used for comparison is the delivered reliability of the program. They consider sampling over the input domain without the aspect of software correction. Hence, the impact of corrections is also missing from these models. The models presented in this paper consider the actual testing scenario, which involves the impact of changes made on the software over a period of time. Notice that most of the earlier models used in efficacy studies do not have the time dimension because they deal with a fixed number of inputs from the input domain without the aspect of software correction or change.

Srivastava (2009) explained about path testing, which searches the program domain for suitable test cases that covers every possible path in the Software under Test (SUT). It is a stronger criterion when compared to statement and branch coverage criteria. This proposed work used to increase the chances of error detection and increase the coverage. In general, it is impossible to achieve this goal, a program may contain an infinite number of paths and is exponential to the number of branches in it and many of them may be unfeasible. Finally, the numbers of test cases are too large, since each path can be covered by several test cases. For these reasons, path testing becomes a NP complete problem, since there is necessity in covering all possible paths computationally, which is impractical.

SUMMARY OF THE SURVEY

In this literature survey, the structural testing on conventional application studies shows that the branch coverage is a superset of statement coverage, which examines all parts of the program. Branches in the given program are the key elements in the branch coverage, which needs more importance on branches. Branch coverage condition has a high potential value with respect to the software evaluation process in the software area. Hence in the proposed work GASE examines all parts of the program, only by evaluating branches, the feasible branches are covered to achieve high branch coverage.

The works related to structural testing on web applications describe the challenges for modelling web application testing methods. Web application testing framework proposed in this book, is with NOPET and Pareto optimality concepts which considers number of tasks involved in test cases. Many test cases have the same number of operands (tasks), and then estimated execution time which is considered as a tie breaker. Then the critical test cases are passed to the Pareto optimality framework which resolves conflicts when it comes to multiple objectives like execution cost, statement coverage and the time of recent modification of web pages. Finally, it will automate the execution of test cases in a parallel manner in cloud environment by simulating the working of web pages using selenium and sauce labs across different environments and browsers.

The structural testing on cloud applications survey demonstrates that multi-tenancy plays a significant role on software as a service (SaaS). Structure of SaaS multi-tenant cloud aware applications initiates several new challenges with the central one being a tenant. In cloud testing, tenant applications are tested to analyse the performance of each tenant. At the same time, numerous performance-testing techniques exist; most of them produce only fixed progressions of test configurations. This work addresses the challenges on Multi-tenancy testing in SaaS and considers the configuration dynamically, whereby SaaS testing differs from testing conventional applications.

III

STRUCTURAL TESTING APPROACHES

STRUCTURAL TESTING APPROACHES FOR CONVENTIONAL AND CLOUD BASED APPLICATIONS

Software testing is important during development phase to point out the defects and errors to make sure the reliability, performance and satisfaction of the customer in the application. Software testing is necessary to provide customer facilities to deliver high quality software's or applications, which needs lower maintenance cost and an effective performance. The proposed book is implemented in three ways for testing conventional and cloud applications. Initially the proposed work on testing is for conventional applications where GASE (Genetic algorithm and symbolic execution) is developed, which achieves high branch coverage over object oriented programs thereby, while testing improves the testing performance. Then the book focuses on web applications testing where the test cases are ordered so that maximum faults are detected in minimal amount of time. The critical test cases, identifies more faults in web applications, prioritizing the test cases which helps in testing web applications in minimal time. Finally, performance testing is on Multi-tenant SaaS cloud over social media applications, in cloud environment. Hence, the proposed work aims to improve the performance testing for conventional applications as well as applications on cloud and social media environment.

STRUCTURAL TESTING FOR CONVENTIONAL BASED APPLICATIONS

In software industry, for structural testing of programs generating test cases is an important task. Software testing to achieve high branch coverage needs some execution details for the software developers. Structural testing based test data generation has made progress in recent years for all categories of conventional applications.

Genetic Algorithm and Symbolic Execution for structural testing refinement

In a program, during software testing it is impossible to run all statements or branches. Generating a set of feasible paths to achieve high branch coverage needs more attention. The GASE in the proposed work addresses the challenges. In software testing, automation testing is the key factor because testing is very expensive task in terms of time and human effort. An important technique used in testing software is structural testing, in which a particular type of program element is selected for branch coverage. The dynamic test data generation in structural testing is the mostly applied approach for generating test cases because the generation is guided by the execution of the code under test. The amount of completion attained by any set of test cases, known as coverage, reflects the percentage of exercised structural elements such as branches, paths, etc. In traditional approach, the numbers of feasible and infeasible paths of the code are not known. Whereas, in structural testing test coverage is calculated in terms of structural or data-flow units that have been implemented.

These structural or dataflow units can be statements, branches, etc. Statement or block coverage is the fraction of the total number of statements that have been executed by the test data. Branch coverage is the fraction of the total number of branches that have been executed. In a program, the value of the variable is modified without the variable being modified along every path. Decision coverage is also known as branch coverage. Whenever there are two or more possible exits present from the statement, it is known as branch. These statements have two outcomes, either TRUE or FALSE. With the loop control statement like DO-WHILE or IF statement in a program, the outcome of the statement is either TRUE or FALSE and branch coverage ensures that each outcome i.e. TRUE and FALSE of control statement has been executed at least once. Otherwise, can say that control statement IF has been evaluated both to TRUE and FALSE statements.

The formula to calculate branch coverage is: Branch Coverage = ((Number of branch outcomes executed / Total number of branch outcomes) *100 %). In structural testing, branch coverage measures the execution of independent code segments. Independent code segments are sections of code that have no branches inside or outside of them. In an additional technique, an independent code segment is a section of code that you would anticipate to implement in its entirety each time its run. Research in industries has shown that even if functional testing has been done it only achieves 60% to 90% branch coverage in software testing. Branch coverage is stronger than statement coverage and it requires more test cases to achieve 100% branch coverage. The goal of this research is to improve existing structural testing techniques that use evolutionary computing techniques like evolutionary algorithms, swarm intelligence, random testing, genetic algorithm etc., for test case generation and constraint solving for computing concrete test data. This work mainly focuses on branch coverage structural testing based on genetic algorithm. The existing technique used in the branch coverage testing of software requires large computational cost and complex algebraic manipulations.

In this work, a novel approach GASE is proposed to increase the branch coverage efficiency. GASE algorithm integrates genetic algorithm and symbolic execution to generate test cases automatically to satisfy predefined testing standard. These standards have been set by the necessities for test data set satisfactory of structural testing to achieve high branch coverage. The test data generation is initiated with a randomly chosen input from the input domain of the program. From this initial input a new input is derived in a challenge to strengthen execution in the course of any of the paths through the selected branch.Every individual can collect a measure of its fitness in the environment, which guides the reproduction. Recombination and mutation disturb those individuals, provided that general heuristics is used for searching. Selected individuals are reproduced and the information's are exchanged in pair-wise order to produce new individuals. This information exchange is called crossover. Two selected individuals are combined by creating two new individuals. A small change made in individuals during mutation for newly created individual. Finally, the individuals are then evaluated through the fitness function. In this fitness function measures how well the chromosome satisfies the test criterion. The implementation of GA involves the following cycle:

Selection: In biological evolution, only the fittest survive and their gene pool contributes to the creation of the next generation. Selection in GA is also based on the similar process. During fitness selection, each chromosome is being selected as a good one is proportional to its fitness value.

Alteration to improve good solutions: The alteration step in the genetic algorithm improves the good solution from the present generation to yield the next generation of applicant solutions by performing crossover and mutation.

Crossover: Crossover may be observed as artificial reproduction in which chromosomes from two individuals are mutual to create the chromosome for the following generations. This is done by merging two chromosomes from two different solutions at a crossover point and exchanging the merged parts. The knowledge gained from this is that some genes with good features from one chromosome may act as an outcome combining with some good genes in the other chromosome to generate a better resolution characterized by the new chromosome.

Mutation: Mutation is a random modification in the genetic composition. It is beneficial for presenting new characteristics in a population, those that not only reaches through crossover alone. Crossover only reorders existing characteristics to give new combinations. For example, if the primary bit in every chromosome of a generation occurs to be 1, any new chromosome shaped through crossover will also have 1 as the first bit.

The mutation operator slightly changes the current individual values to another one gene, 0 bit to a 1 or vice versa. Although it is useful for introducing new traits in the solution pool, mutations can be counterproductive and can be applied only infrequently and randomly.

Evaluate: Evaluating the fitness of all the individuals in the population (fitness may be thought as the inverse of an objective function that has to be minimized. Fitness function values should get increased during path optimization process). Create a new population by performing the operations (crossover, reproduction, and mutation) on individuals with high fitness values. Discard the old population and iterate using the new population was iteration, referred to as a generation.

Symbolic Execution, also called as symbolic evaluation is a program analyser that determines which inputs cause each part of a program to execute. This has been used to create high code coverage test suites which automatically identify bugs and to signify inputs as symbolic values in place of its concrete values. When describing a branch whose condition contains symbolic values, where two paths are created, the matching constraints are added to each path. In symbolic execution, once the execution of a path dismisses the execution path, constraint collections are used to create concrete inputs that are used in the paths as defined below.

Symbolic State: <symbolic_binding, execution_path, path_condition>

Symbolic State:

Symbolic Execution rules: In Read (x) remove any existing binding for x and add binding x = X, where X is a newly introduced symbol. In Write (expression), the output (n) = computed _ symbolic _ value_expression (n counter initialized to 1 and automatically incremented after each write statement). Where x: = expression to construct symbolic value of expression SV; replace existing binding of x with x = SV. After execution of a statement of a path that corresponds to an edge of control graph, append the edge to execution path.

The objective of solving a symbolic regression problem is finding a function that closely matches some unknown function on a certain interval. From that, symbolic execution can help to improve the method arguments in method sequences initially generated by genetic algorithm. GASE algorithm acts like a bridge connecting GA (genetic algorithm) and SE (symbolic execution) by programming actual tests generated by symbolic execution as chromosomes; these chromosomes are the population individuals for evolutionary testing to progress. GASE framework implemented in the proposed work is applied to test 13 classes previously used in evaluating white-box test generation tools. The experimental result shows that this proposed framework could achieve higher branch coverage than any other branch coverage tools in structural testing.

Fitness generations

A typical GA is mathematically expressed in equation.

Fitness = Error rate (accuracy) + number of individuals + majority classification made by rules in an individual + coverage.

In the fitness function equation, the first part of expression is the percentage of coverage for the gene that considers the total number of paths that have to be covered according to the selected criterion. The second and third parts of the fitness function may be considered as a kind of reward to the chromosome. These are introduced based on the observations that a chromosome which only covers already covered paths, (in a former or the current generation) cannot be a step towards optimization. The second part of the fitness function gives the true contribution of the chromosome in terms of covering the targeted paths. The percentage of the paths covered for the first time by the chromosome under investigation is more important than the total number of paths covered. The final part of equation rewards chromosomes that achieve coverage of rarely covered paths.

A path that is not covered by a lot of possible solutions might have exclusivity requiring special conditions from the input variables and those conditions may have particular relation between the input variables (for example relationship conditions be 0 and the other less than a specific value, or the first variable must be twice the value of the second one, etc.). Chromosomes that achieve coverage of those paths are rewarded. The proposed GASE Genetic algorithm bridging symbolic execution [b] into the fitness function for branch coverage methodology reduces the number of fitness evaluations required to cover a high branch as shown in algorithm1. In the branch distance, the range [0, 1] of a Boolean branch conditions is obtained based on the evaluation of the boundary condition. Values close to 1 indicate that the condition is far from being satisfied whereas; value zero indicates that the condition falls nearer. Intermediate values smoothly guide the search towards satisfying the condition. In the path, distance is the sum of the branch distances computed for the conditions that appears to be non-destroyed in the path condition of the approximated path expression. At the point when all conjuncts in the way condition ascertain to genuine when it is zero. The approximation level is the number of conditions that are dropped from the path condition as they involve variables defined inside loops that are used in the condition.

Performance analysis of GASE algorithm

In order to determine the appropriate size of search space, the genetic algorithm and symbolic execution were scripted using Scheme functions. These scripts represent research prototypes; a manual checking is performed based on the results obtained. To ensure that the test had correctly identified the variables that could potentially affect the predicates of interest and another source of bias comes from the selection of the programs to be studied. These impacts upon the external validity of the empirical study, those extents to which it is possible to generalize from the results obtained. Typically, it is impossible to sample a sufficiently large set of programs such that the full diversity of all possible programs could be captured. The rich and diverse nature of programs makes this as an unrealistic goal. However, it is possible, a variety of programming styles and sources have been used. These analyses draw upon code from real world programs, both from industrial production code and from open source. Furthermore, it should be noted that the number of different branches considered in 13 classes, provide a relatively large pool of subjects from which observations are made.

However, attention is required before making any claims, whether these results would be observed on other programs, possibly from different sources and in different programming languages. The experiments reveal that search techniques are commonly used in Search-Based Software Testing, complete with their usual parameter settings; but likewise, care should be taken in generalizing the results to their respective families (local search, genetic algorithms, etc.,) as a whole.

As with all such experimental software engineering, further experiments are required in order to replicate the results contained here. However, these results show that cases do indeed exist where there is a statistically significant relationship between search space reduction and improved performance of search algorithms for test data generation. The structural testing in this work GASE use automated execution of test cases by means of genetic algorithm and symbolic execution.

Algorithm 1: GASE Algorithm

1.[Start] Generate random population of p1+p2+...pn Chromosomes (Suitable solutions for the problem)

2.[Fitness] Evaluate the fitness ffn of each chromosome pi.

3.[Population] Create a new population.

4.[Selection] Select two parent chromosomes from a population according to their fitness.

5.[Crossover] Cross over the parents to form a new offspring.

6.[Mutation] Mutate new offspring at each locus.

7.[Accepting] Place new offspring in a new population

8.[Replace] Use new generated population for a further run of Algorithm

9.[Test]Stop, if the end condition is satisfied.

10.[Classify] These variables will be treated as symbolic variables during symbolic execution.

11.[Implement]Instrument the program.

12.[Choose] Choose an arbitrary input to begin with.

13.[Execute] Execute the program.

14.[Re-Execute]Generate a set of symbolic constraints to re-execute the program symbolically which also include path conditions.

15.[Reverse] Negate the last path condition, which is not already negated in order to visit a new execution path. The algorithm terminates when there is no path condition.

16.[Invoke] Invoke an automated theorem proves to generate a new input. Return to step 15, if there is no input satisfying the constraints.

17.[Return] Return to step 13.

In GASE algorithm, genetic algorithm is integrated with symbolic execution. In which individuals of population measure the fitness. Recombination and mutation are done for these individuals, the information is exchanged with the help of crossover and mutation to each newly created individuals. Fitness functions are then evaluated for newly created individuals. The implementation of GA involves the following cycle:

Evaluate the fitness of all of the individuals in the population (fitness may be thought about as the inverse of an objective function that has to be minimized, fitness function values should increase during the optimization process). Create a new population by performing operations (crossover, reproduction, and mutation) on the individuals with high fitness values. Remove the old population and repeat using the new population.

GASE framework:

GASE framework is implemented as a tool for testing Java programs. GASE framework is effective in generating tests to achieve higher branch coverage than the existing test generation tools. GASE test effectiveness is compared in terms of branch coverage with widely existing test generation tools. Evolutionary testing tool is selected for object-oriented programs. jCUTE, which tests Java classes using the dynamic symbolic execution technique.

STRUCTURAL TESTING FOR WEB BASED APPLICATIONS

A framework for web applications testing is developed to order the test cases so that maximum faults can be detected in minimal amount of time. The critical test cases that cause more faults in web applications are identified. Detecting the critical test cases in web applications is essential in some of the crucial situations like when the tester needs to have minimum execution time or halt the running application in between.

A prioritization and parallelization model is developed in order to identify critical test cases so as to detect more faults in minimal amount of time. The identification of critical test cases is based on the number of operands present in the test cases. This process is parallelized using map reduce framework in order to have minimum execution time.

There exist multiple objectives among the test cases with equal importance producing conflicts. In order to have a balanced optimality, a multi objective optimization technique called Pareto optimality is used. A ranking model is used to rank test cases considering statement coverage, execution cost and recent updating which have equal importance. The test cases are dynamically invoked using TestNG framework with selenium using java. The test cases are finally simulated over sauce labs which is the cloud environment providing test results in the form of videos, log files, screenshots and metadata. Sauce labs also enable us to perform concurrent execution of test cases.

Improving Test Case Prioritization using NOPET algorithm

Web application testing is a technique of software testing used to test the web applications where the user interface and the major functions of the web pages are tested. The web application should be tested completely to ensure that it is working properly before hosting it on live. This testing allows checking whether the web application can tolerate the hardware sufficiency in the server, user traffic and so on. This also finds the bottleneck in the systems before they occur in production environment.

Web application testing over cloud uses cloud infrastructure. Testing organizations have more challenges such as more test cases, high payments per test, low-test budget and no reuse of tests. To ensure high quality and to avoid outages, testing should be done within and outside the data . Unlike traditional on-premises testing environment, cloud testing provides users pay-per-use pricing, flexibility and reduced time. Manual web application testing is not time efficient therefore testing environment should be automated in order to test the application efficiently. When this automated testing is carried out in cloud, it is an added advantage, as it minimizes cost, time and resources. Hence, the proposed system is used in testing of web applications prior to its deployment by using cloud environment with prioritization, parallelization and pareto-optimality ranking approach. To develop an automated testing framework for web applications over cloud environment using Parallelization (simultaneous execution of multiple tasks is required).

The main techniques used in the proposed system are parallelization of the test cases. The process of identification of critical test cases is parallelized using map reduce framework to reduce the time consumed significantly as independent tasks in prioritization technique are executed concurrently. The NOPET (Number of Operands Parallelization Execution Time) algorithm is imposed on the test cases and the test cases are ordered based on the number of operands considering the execution time as a tie-breaker.

Web application test cases are written in java with the help of built-in functions of the packages imported by installing the selenium. The idea is to execute the test cases in prioritized order at the run time dynamically. Since dynamic binding is implemented rather than static binding, java reflection concept must be incorporated so that the test cases are called during the run time so that late binding is achieved.

In case, there is a tie between two test cases, that is, when both test cases involve the same number of operands, then the execution time is taken as a tie breaker. Sauce labs are in cloud environment, when it is used to simulate different operating system and browsers to check whether the webpage is capable of functioning in cross platform and cross browsers. Statement coverage, recent updating and execution cost of a test case are also a vital part in testing and are of equal importance. A concept known as Pareto optimality is used in order to achieve balanced coverage of multiple objectives and to prioritize the critical test cases that are found in NOPET algorithm.

To commence with, the class name of the test cases written and the method names corresponding to the classes are stored in ordered series, same as the order in which it is fed to the testing framework. In order to identify the critical test cases, the specific number of operands be calculated and this task must be done simultaneously in order to minimize the expected time. Hence comes the map reduce framework involving parallelization (concurrent execution of independent tasks) to pre-determine the number of tasks involved. Consequently, the test cases are sorted based on the number of operands in it using map reduce framework and most critical test cases are identified.

Identifying quantity of operands in test cases using parallelization: Web pages form the integral part of the web applications. The test cases written for web pages are taken as input for testing framework. Web test cases consist of several operands that are used to form the basic functionality of each test case. Test cases are sorted and ordered based on the number of operands in each test case. The quantity of operands in each test case is identified by parallelization utilizing the map reduce framework. The mapper class takes the operands in the test cases as the key and aggregated values are evaluated in the reduce class.

Test case optimization using Pareto optimality: Pareto optimality is used to provide balanced coverage when there are multiple conflicting objectives that have equal importance. The objectives considered for Pareto optimality are statement coverage, recent updating and execution cost. The web page which has undergone recent updating will suffer from compatibility issues with the remaining web pages or with the environment. The execution cost of the test cases is computed using the total number of statements involved in it. There is a chance of finding more faults in a test case involving not only number of tasks but also maximum statements which constitute the execution cost. The statement coverage is evaluated with the executed statements in a test case.

Pareto optimality of the test cases with multiple conflicting objectives is analyzed using utopia and nadir points. The utopia point referring to the most desirable point is detected using the following objectives: minimum updating time, maximum execution cost, and maximum statement coverage. The nadir point is computed using the following objectives: maximum updating time, minimum execution cost, and minimum statement coverage. The test cases are ordered based on how much close they are to the utopia point and far from the nadir point.

The test cases are executed automatically producing minimal execution time. The testers will not know which classes and methods to run during compile time. Hence, the execution of test cases is automated at run time using dynamic invocation and java reflection in the classes present in the test cases. The test cases are simulated over sauce labs. Sauce labs are used to provide cross browser grid for executing selenium web driver tests. It provides over 385 browsers, OS, device configurations. Hence Sauce labs are used for automated testing, also social applications over cloud is tested. Currently, many users around the world use social applications like Face book, YouTube in their day today life for communication, enlightenment and entertainment. These social applications tend to have more problems since they are updated daily. So these applications are tested over cloud environment by designing the test cases and prioritizing them using NOPET algorithm with Pareto optimality and run over sauce labs.

Critical test case identification

Test cases are designed with several operands from the web pages in the web applications. The operands in test cases are essential for identifying the faults in the web pages since the operands define the major functionality of the test cases. The web application test cases are given as input to the NOPET (Number of Operands Parallelization Execution Time) algorithm. The test cases are fed into the parallelization framework. The quantity of operands in each test case is calculated by map reduce. The input test cases are analyzed and are sorted based on the number of operands present in it using NOPET algorithm.

In case if any two test cases exist having the same number of operands; the execution cost for the test case is used as the tie-breaker. The execution time is calculated for a sample test case which involves a major task. The execution cost for each operand in a test case is computed by the product of quantity of the operand and the sample execution time that is calculated in prior. Finally, the critical test cases are identified after sorting the input test cases based on the number of operands.

Identification of critical test cases is essential for finding more faults in the web applications. Test cases are said to be critical, if they involve major functionalities, or when the tester has less amount of time for execution and needs to run the main test cases, or when the tester needs to halt the running application in between. The critical test cases are based on the testers to decide during the run time which test cases are important and deduct more faults. The critical test cases are then balanced optimally using Pareto optimality approach where the conflicting objectives, statement coverage, execution cost and recent updating have equal importance.

STRUCTURAL TESTING FOR CLOUD BASED APPLICATIONS

This section focuses on the system design and implementation of proposed multi-tenancy cloud platform, which could be used for finding performance testing and fittest function of each tenant. Contents in this section consist of discussions about the system modules such as multi-tenancy architecture, performance testing using GASE algorithm.

In SaaS Multi-tenancy section, this book gives a short summary of the most significant architectural aspects that are connected to this research in addition to the contact of multi-tenancy on probable standard and metrics. In cloud computing, multi-tenancy is defined as a technology in which more number of customers is also known as tenants, share a single instance of a software application. In addition, every tenant is able to modify the application for his own specific needs but the application's core code remains same.

Multitenant Testing

SaaS Multi-tenancy architecture deals with the most significant aspects that are connected to this book in addition to the contact of multi-tenancy on probable standard and metrics. In cloud computing, multi-tenancy is defined as a technology in which more number of customers is also known as tenants, share a single instance of a software application. In addition, every tenant is able to modify the application for his own specific needs but the application's core code remains same.

Accessing the setup and creating tenant:

When a request arrives, the specific cloud client has to be known and the customer (tenant) fits into different approaches be in attendance to classify the tenant. One key is to connect the tenant's specific information to identify the client's information. On the other hand, multi-tenant moves towards the necessity of user authentication in addition to duplicate user names in different tenants being not possible therefore breach segregation occurs. Therefore, the tenant identification is achievable exclusive of involving a login as well as a photocopy in which user names are sustained. In this book the frequent approach is to relocate the tenant's identifier at the time of the implementation which controls the thread context, to which the significant data is emotionally involved.

SaaS multi-tenant network:

The meaning of multi-tenancy architecture has become wider because of new service models that take the benefit of virtualization and remote access in cloud computing environment. A software-as-a-service (SaaS) provider has one instance of its application that runs on one instance of a database and provides web right to use for multiple customers. Each tenant's information is inaccessible, remains indistinguishable to other tenants. Tenant accesses a single instance of the SaaS application and all the tenants are provided this software instance and hardware infrastructure. They feel that this software is dedicated software serving their needs over the internet. We know that multiple clients organize the identical instance of software and all data is housed in a multi-tenant database.

Individual tenants may have restricted or no capability to make personalized modifications on functionality. This does not imply that the functionality itself is limited, but rather it is more difficult to customize. As such, a multi-tenant solution is suited to companies without any requirement for insignificant or most important software alteration or reconfiguration. In multi-tenancy architecture, this type of standardization is an advantage to companies who employ software out of the box. Most reputable SaaS cloud hosting providers are very good at anticipating their customers' needs, and will offer the most-relevant software applications in the standardized version. Sometimes a multi-tenant application is set up for a chosen group of customers to give these users access for pre-release versions of applications. Often beta versions are given access to users for testing purposes.

External connectivity and security policies:

Usually the executed persistence application protocol interface of the platform or the SaaS cloud application development engineer has to make sure that the partition of information using SQL statements with tenant ID and tenant specific accumulation strength are being essential. The tenant identification may be based on an identity management system which is a part of the metadata manager. On the other hand, application contact might agree to run assault from one to other tenants with unrestricted rights in addition to its being replicated by individual actions like SQL encoding and stack over flow prevention.

SaaS multi-tenant testing:

Multiple tenants share same resources and hardware utilization is also advanced on average and it is essential to make sure that all the tenants utilize the same resources as per their requirements. The application has to be highly scalable and must perform well with the provided resources. In general terms, if one tenant blocks major portion of the resources then the other tenant's performance will not be affected. To find the performance and scalability performance testing tools are used like JMeter, Load Runner. Policies and metadata are used to generate test cases for testing SaaS application, and the testing can be embedded in the cloud computing platform where tenant applications are run.

Tenant based fault / disaster recovery testing:

This testing can be used to test SaaS applications by implanting fixed test case creation with the database connected with a tenant. Test cases can be selected to test the SaaS applications continuously. If a test script detects a failure, the ranking of the test script with its associated test cases will be increased so that it will be used early and more often in continuous testing. The cloud platform can run those test scripts continuously by selecting most potent test case with dynamic ranking of test cases.

Tenant based performance testing:

In software testing, the system testing is defined as the testing, which tests the system as a whole. This System testing obtains all the integrated modules of the different components from the integration testing phase. Also it combines all of the unusual parts into a system which is then tested to check and remove, if any errors or bugs found. In this process the system will check tenant-based system QoS requirements for errors and also verifies the reliability, performance, availability, security, connectivity etc.

Tenant based multi-tenant testing:

In multi-tenant application both functional and non-functional testing has to be done. When moving outside functional and non-functional, testing the multi-tenant application for configurable and non-configurable components moved across tenants, application up-gradation scenarios. In this, functional testing includes automated regression testing, exploratory testing, data migration & data integration testing and checklist testing. Non-functional testing supports security testing and performance testing. But moving beyond functional and non-functional testing is a sign of prominence and it also needs to be laid on testing the organized features like compatibility testing, live testing etc., of the SaaS application.

Service component unit testing:

Service component unit testing needs testing engineers to carry out both black-box and white-box unit tests for quality assurance of SaaS service components. Testing smallest testable parts of software is called Unit Testing; Component Testing, also known as Module or Program testing, identifies flaws in individual components or modules of the application. This ensures debugging at the earliest possible stage before the SDLC (Software Development Life Cycle) advances. It follows unit testing and precedes integration testing. In-house component and unit testing may end up consuming a lot of time, money and resources as well as leads to a considerable deviation from the core business goals. Authorising non-core activities such as component testing of software applications to an experienced and reliable testing services provider would be a pragmatic solution for businesses: it ensures quality product with low cost and also reduce overheads in speedy software development.

Instance based performance testing:

If the framework provisioning policy decides that a new server is needed, it will connect to the cloud interface requesting a new instance. The cloud interface checks whether the user can request new instances and if there are any free resources to start the instance. If all the conditions are suitable, a new virtual machine is started in the cloud and the instance ID is sent back to the framework.

SaaS Multitenant Performance Testing Over Social Networks

Cloud Services Technology can be considered as the key technology for creation of Cloud Services. In modern years, cloud computing client has an advantage due to the lower expenses with improved elasticity in a well-organized and scalable manner in addition to the cloud client's expense on a short-term pay per use basis. In Cloud Computing Multi-tenant SaaS applications organize the implementation system on multiple servers in a circulated technique. Multi-tenancy is defined as a single instance of the software run, which takes place in the service provider's infrastructure and simultaneously multiple tenant access the same hardware resources. At the same time multi-tenancy is the organizational entity, which allows tenants to organize the SaaS application in the direction fitting their needs as if it runs on a complete location.

In cloud environment tenant groups have a number of users which are the stake holders in the society. The reimbursement of the multi-tenant model is the deployment of application which fetches easily for the cloud service provided. Also, multiple tenants are shared through same hardware resources; as a result, operation speed of the hardware can be improved. Instead of installing hundreds of application instance, only one instance can be installed. Hence, it leads to the condensation of the overall costs of the application. There are different SaaS developments levels that are being introduced in this Open Stack multi-tenancy cloud computing environment and relates to how the multi-tenancy cloud SaaS application is delivered to many tenants (customers).In this first stage of mutitenancy, each customer has its individual SaaS application, which is customizable. In this, on host server every customer runs its own instance of the application. In the second level, each tenant has a separate instance of the application on the vendor host. In the third level, the vendor runs a single instance that provides each customer with configurable metadata. Besides, it also provides a single user experience and feature for each customer. In the fourth and final level of multi-tenancy, multiple customers on a load-balanced farm of the same instances through each tenant's data are kept separate.

In this proposed study the performance testing is measured on multiple tenants over social networks. After the performance testing is done on tenants, their results are recorded in a separate excel sheet. This excel sheet values are used for fitness function using GASE algorithm for obtaining the best of each tenant. In multi-tenant performance testing a tenant performance, evaluation report and scalability analysis report for cloud SaaS applications are done. In addition to cloud computing, systems need trustworthy reproduction explanations and surroundings to continue large test simulation and execution.

Performance test tracking infrastructure for SaaS follows and reports SaaS testing performance data and attributes, including performance, reliability, scalability, and throughputs. On-demand large-scale performance test simulation allows users to select the accessible performance test script test & load test script set with the corresponding test tool for performance testing. Users can select a predefined validation model with metrics or the users can go to an additional screen to classify their performance evaluation metrics.

Performance analysis of multi-tenants

In the large-scale performance testing, a user can generate a preferred number of performance test agents, concerning preselected performance loads & auto tests. SaaS performance testing and evaluation is to support non-functional testing of SaaS application. The proposed system uses the graphic model and metrics. It is a graphical process of displaying multiple data in the outline of a three dimensional chart of three or more quantitative variables being described that starts from the same point axes. In addition, the relative position and angle of the axes is typically uninformative. Based on this performance-testing model, a set of metrics are developed using genetic algorithm and symbolic execution, they are implemented and tested to support SaaS monitoring and evaluation of numerous quantitative performance, scalability parameters and indicators.

Symbolic execution consists of the systematic exploration of this execution tree. Each inner node is a branching conclusion and every leaf is a program state that includes its own address space, program counter, and set of constraints on program variables. When an execution encounters a testing goal, the constraints collected from the root to the goal leaf can be solved to produce concrete program inputs that exercise the path to the testing goal (bug). Thus, symbolic execution is significantly more resourceful than extensive input based testing and equally complete. In a cloud computing setting, organization parallel symbolic execution additionally has the need to cope with frequent fluctuation in resource quality, accessibility, cost etc. Machines have variable performance characteristics, their network proximity to each other is unpredictable, and failures are frequent. A system like Open stack must therefore cope with these problems and the essential challenge of parallel symbolic execution.

C2IST - INTEGRATED STRUCTURAL TESTING

Software testing is one of the important actions in software development. It regulates the correctness, completeness and quality of the software product or component. In general, software testing is done inside using the infrastructure that occurs within the organization and software testing function has become an interesting activity for enterprises due to increasing technological difficulties, software challenges, high costs to simulate and security. Due to the rising complexity of business applications, it is harder to build and sustain in-house testing services that impersonate real-time environments. Cloud computing is opening up new panoramas of opportunity for software testing. While comparing with traditional testing in terms of maintaining an in-house test environment, cloud based testing offers a convincing combination of pay-peruse, low costs and elimination of open capital expenses. The benefits, however, extend outside the cost and also the non-cost factors contain utility like, freedom from holding assets, enhanced collaboration, on-demand flexibility, and greater levels of efficiency. Most significantly, it reduces time-to-market for key business applications. Cloud-based testing introduces a new set of challenges, such as data security and a lack of standards, especially in the public cloud model.

Software testing is not a single action but a sequence of scheduled tasks that need to be implemented along with the software development actions to ensure that a product is delivered without any faults. Conventional testing can be done in two ways

i.Manual testing

ii.Automated testing using tools.

Web Application Testing is defined as a process of testing the web applications to find the possible bugs before the code is moved into the production environment.

The following testing activities are generally carried out for testing web applications.

i. Functional Testing

ii. Usability testing

iii. Interface testing

iv. Compatibility testing

iv. Performance testing

v. Security testing

Software testing is important during development phase to point out the defects and errors to ensure the reliability, performance and satisfaction of the customer in the application. Software testing is necessary to provide customer facilities to delivery high quality software's or applications, which needs lower maintenance cost and an effective performance.

The proposed (C2IST) is implemented in three ways: In the first work, high branch coverage is achieved over object-oriented programs using search based structural testing algorithms called GASE algorithm. A genetic algorithm (or GA) is a search technique used in computing to find true or approximate solutions for optimization and search problems. Genetic algorithms are categorized as global search heuristics. In evolutionary algorithms, genetic algorithm plays a vital role that use approaches enthused by evolutionary computing such as inheritance, mutation, selection, and crossover (also called recombination). In the evolution stage randomly generated individual population are selected which happens in generations.

In this genetic algorithm, an individual fitness is calculated in each population generation and multiple individuals are selected from the current population (based on their fitness), and modified (recombined and possibly mutated) to form a new population. For the next iteration the newly generated population is used. When a maximum number of generations have been formed or a satisfactory fitness level has been reached for the population, the algorithm ends. If the algorithm has been terminated due to a maximum number of generations, a satisfactory solution may or may not have been reached. In software testing the symbolic execution is useful to help the generation of test data and it demonstrates the program quality. Selections of paths that are exercised by a set of data values are required for execution. At the point when a real information is executed which results in the yield of a progression of qualities.

In symbolic execution, the data is replaced by symbolic values with a set of expressions, one expression per output variable. The common method for symbolic execution is to complete a program analysis, resulting in the creation of a flow graph. Symbolic Execution is also called symbolic evaluation. Program analyser determines which inputs cause each part of a program to execute. It has been used to create high code coverage test suites automatically to identify bugs and to signify inputs as symbolic values in place of its concrete values. When describing a branch whose condition contains symbolic values, where two paths are created and the matching constraints are added to each path. In symbolic execution, once the executions of a path end, the execution path and constraint collections are used to create concrete inputs that are used in the paths.

In the second book tenant's performance, testing is analyzed on Multi-tenant SaaS cloud over social media applications. The evaluation report and scalability analysis report for cloud SaaS applications are done. Performance test tracking infrastructure for SaaS follows and reports SaaS testing performance data and attributes, including performance, reliability, scalability, and throughputs. On-demand large-scale performance test simulation allows users to select the accessible performance test script test & load test script set with the corresponding test tool for performance testing. Users can select a predefined validation model with metrics or the users can go to an additional screen to classify their performance evaluation metrics.

In the large-scale performance testing, a user can generate a preferred number of performance test agents to pertain preselected performance loads & auto tests. SaaS performance testing and evaluation is to support non-functional testing of SaaS application.

In the third book web applications are developed to order the test cases so that maximum faults can be detected in minimal amount of time. The critical test cases, which cause more faults in web applications, are identified. Web application test cases are written in java with the help of built-in functions of the packages imported by installing the selenium. The idea is to execute the test cases in prioritized order at the run time dynamically. Since dynamic binding is implemented rather than static binding, java reflection concept must be incorporated so that the test cases are called during the run time so that late binding is achieved.

In case, there is a tie between two test cases, that is, when both test cases involve the same number of operands, then the execution time is taken as a tie breaker. Sauce labs are the cloud environment used to simulate different operating system and browsers to check whether the webpage is capable of functioning in cross platform and cross browsers. Statement coverage, recent updating and execution cost of a test case are also a vital part in testing and are of equal importance. In order to have balanced coverage of these multiple objectives, a concept known as Pareto optimality is required in order to achieve balanced coverage of multiple objectives and prioritize the critical test cases that are found in NOPET algorithm.

To commence with, the class name of the test cases is written and the method names corresponding to the classes are stored in ordered series same as the order in which it is fed to the testing framework. In order to identify the critical test cases, the specific number of operands must be calculated and this task must be done simultaneously in order to minimize the expected time. Hence, comes the map reduce framework involving parallelization (concurrent execution of independent tasks) to pre-determine the number of tasks involved. Consequently, the test cases are sorted based on the number of operands in it using map reduce framework and most critical test cases are identified.

IV

CONCLUSION AND FUTURE ENHANCEMENTS

CONCLUSION

This book proposes a framework which aims to address the challenges that exists currently in structural testing techniques. In addition to this, a set of features are also presented which can help us in choosing suitable testing technique in the absence of existing knowledge about the testing techniques statistics. This chapter summarizes the book done and findings besides making suggestions for future direction. Hence the main objective is to achieve performance testing in cloud computing environment for structural testing which involves conventional, cloud and web applications. Hence, an integrated approach framework, which is suitable for all these types of applications, is proposed. This novel approach achieves high fitness and performance over cloud computing environment while testing applications.

The principle for testing is based on ensuring that all branches in the programs are implemented. In the case of loops, the fitness is based on the number of classes required. The class of test data formed is far above the ground, because the tests can be going through the fitness function, to the areas where faults are most likely to be revealed. In structural testing, automation testing is the key factor because testing is a very costly task in terms of time and human effort. In this research a novel approach GASE algorithm to increase the branch coverage efficiency was proposed. In the empirical analysis the work is compared for 13 classes in which 8 of 13 classes GASE achieved higher branch coverage than the existing algorithms. Hence initially, Genetic Algorithm and Symbolic Execution for structural testing refinements carried out to generate test cases automatically and to satisfy predefined testing standard.

Many commercial websites like IRCTC, Flipkart, and Amazon face a lot of issues when deployed in real time. This project when extended in terms of scalability and when it acts as a suggestion provider to the developer about the faults that are more likely to occur, can solve most critical problems at the development stage itself. Test cases (web pages) are designed with several operands which define the major functionality of the web applications. The NOPET algorithm computes the number of operands in each test case using map reduce framework and sorts them based on the operands. Pareto optimality resolves the conflict between multiple objectives in the test cases and test cases are prioritized. The NOPET algorithm's performance is compared with the existing test case prioritization algorithms. The average percentage of faults detected (APFD) has been increased to 50% in NOPET algorithm with Pareto optimality when compared with additional greedy and random ordering algorithm. Hence, it can be concluded that NOPET with Pareto optimality ensures that test cases with most desirable results are ordered earlier than the test cases with least desirable result.

In the forthcoming years, cloud testing will be gaining momentum in which performance testing concerns are one of the major obstacles for multitenant cloud. In multi-tenant performance testing, a tenant's performance, evaluation report for each tenant, and scalability analysis are considered. After this deployment process the service line is

• 31 •

accessible by the tenants as a customizable multi-tenant SaaS application. The proposed GASE algorithm uses the recorded excel sheet values for obtaining the best of each tenant in the form of fitness generation. SaaS multi-tenant testing over social network for cloud applications is carried out. The multi-tenancy plays a significant role on software as a service (SaaS). Performance testing and fittest function of each tenant is done by experimental analysis on Open Stack cloud computing environment for Social applications.

FUTURE WORK

In future more number of testing methods can be used over cloud computing environment to further improve the performance and fitness results. Some of the ways in which future research can be enhanced from the proposed work are, in the present work, while employing GASE algorithm for structural testing 13 classes have been used. In future more than 250 classes can be used for testing for having more accuracy. For testing web applications, social networks with particular reference to Face book, YouTube and shopping cart have been used instead, Amazon may be considered for the real time experimental analysis. Also, SaaS Multitenant Network analyse only one tenant performance to provide improvement in performance testing, in future complete tenant database can be used for analyzing tenant performance.

AUTHOR PROFILES

Dr.M.Parthiban is working as Associate professor in the VSB Engineering College, Karur,He has more than 10 years experience in teaching Engineering.He has published more than 15 papers in reputed scientific journals.
Mr.S.Geerthik is working as Assistant professor in the VSB Engineering College, Karur,He has more than 8 years experience in teaching Engineering.He has published more than 10 papers in reputed scientific journals.
Mr.P.Anbumani is working as Assistant professor in the VSB Engineering College, Karur,He has more than 8 years experience in teaching Engineering.He has published more than 10 papers in reputed scientific journals.